S0-ACB-042

Saving Money

by Natalie M. Rosinsky

Content Adviser: Jaclyn B. H. Finstad, New Ulm, Minnesota;
M.B.A., University of Findlay, Ohio

Reading Adviser: Dr. Alexa Sandmann, Professor of Literacy,
The University of Toledo; Member, International Reading Association

Let's See Library
Compass Point Books
Minneapolis, Minnesota

Compass Point Books
3109 West 50th Street, #115
Minneapolis, MN 55410

Visit Compass Point Books on the Internet at *www.compasspointbooks.com* or e-mail your
request to *custserv@compasspointbooks.com*

On the cover: Twin brother and sister save their money in a big jar.

Photographs ©: Gary Sundermeyer, cover; BananaStock, 4; Stock Montage, 6; Chuck Savage/Corbis, 8; Dan
Dempster/Dembinsky Photo Associates, 10; Peter Beck/Corbis, 14; Unicorn Stock Photos/Jim Shippee, 16;
Spencer Platt/Getty Images, 18; AFP/Corbis, 20; John Cross/The Free Press, 24.

Editor: Catherine Neitge
Photo Researcher: Svetlana Zhurkina
Designers: Melissa Voda/Jaime Martens

Library of Congress Cataloging-in-Publication Data
Rosinsky, Natalie M. (Natalie Myra)
  Saving money / by Natalie M. Rosinsky.
      p. cm. — (Let's see library. Economics) (Let's see library)
  Includes bibliographical references and index.
  ISBN 0-7565-0484-8 (hardcover : alk. paper)
  1. Saving and investment—Juvenile literature. 2. Investments—Juvenile literature. [1. Money. 2. Saving and
investment.] I. Title. II. Series. III. Series: Let's see library
  HC79.S3R674 2004
  332.024—dc21   2002156025

© 2004 by Compass Point Books

All rights reserved. No part of this book may be reproduced without written permission from the publisher. The publisher takes no
responsibility for the use of any of the materials or methods described in this book, nor for the products thereof.
Printed in the United States of America.

Table of Contents

NOTE: In this book, words that are defined in the glossary
*are in **bold** the first time they appear in the text.*

Why Do People Save Money?

Are you going to a wedding soon? You will want new clothes or fancy shoes then! This is a short-term **expense.** Were your boots tight last winter? If so, you can plan on buying new boots next year. This is a long-term expense. People save money for both kinds of expenses. They also try to have money saved for unplanned problems. Losing a job is one such emergency.

Some families save for many years to pay for college. Money that is not spent or paid in **taxes** may be saved.

◄ *A mother saves money to spend on her daughter's new dress.*

How Have People Saved Money?

Long ago, people hid their savings. They buried coins and other treasures in the ground. They placed their savings under buildings.

Often, when people traveled, they brought their savings along. Thieves sometimes took money from travelers. Rich people decided to leave their money at home!

They still wanted to buy things, though. These travelers began to leave their money with someone else. This person, called a banker, would write a note. It told the amount of the **deposit.** Travelers used these notes like money. The banker was paid for keeping money safe until it was needed.

◀ *Pirates buried their treasure to keep it safe. Rich people hid their savings, too.*

How Do People Save Money Today?

Most people keep their savings in a bank. Today, banks are businesses with many workers. The bank records each person's deposits and **withdrawals** of money. It sends regular **statements** about the account. The statements also list the **interest** the account has earned. Interest is money the bank adds to the account.

Different banks offer different rates of interest to savers. Many people choose the bank offering the most interest. Some people choose the bank closest to home or work.

Banks earn money by making **loans.** They charge borrowers higher interest rates than they give savers.

◄ *Customers wait in line at a bank.*

What are Some U.S. Laws About Banks?

Is someone's money safe in a bank today? Yes, indeed!

Banks must keep careful records. When making loans, they must be honest and use good sense. Banks must also keep enough money in **reserve** for withdrawals. The government makes certain these laws are followed. Since 1913, its Federal Reserve Bank System has checked on banks regularly.

In 1933, the United States began to protect savings in another way. It **insures** most bank accounts up to $100,000. Banks must tell people if they belong to the Federal Deposit Insurance Corporation (FDIC).

◄ *A boy makes a deposit at a bank that belongs to the FDIC.*

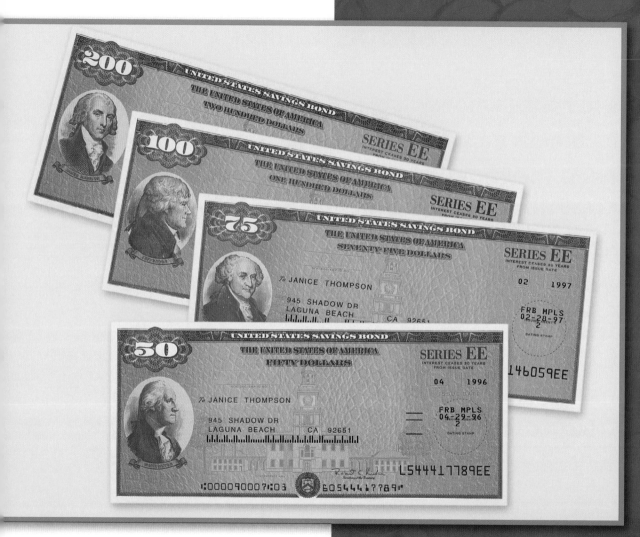

What are Some Other Ways to Save Money?

Some people deposit their savings elsewhere. Instead of a bank, some people use a **credit union.** Some people deposit their money in companies called **savings and loan associations.**

People may depend on the government to help them save. Sometimes, they buy U.S. savings **bonds.** A savings bond is really a long-term loan someone makes to the government. It earns interest over many years. Another government program is the Social Security Administration. It taxes people's **wages.** When workers retire, they get regular payments from Social Security.

◄ *Savings bonds earn interest over many years.*

How Can You Save Your Own Money?

Do you own a piggy bank? If you do, you could continue to save your money at home. Try keeping separate piles for short-term and long-term expenses. If you want your savings to earn interest, though, make other plans!

A grown-up family member can help you start a bank account. You may both need to sign bank forms. One bank in Colorado is just for kids! If you will not need your money for several years, think about savings bonds. A grown-up can help you buy these.

◀ *This boy's piggy bank holds lots of coins.*

What Is Investing Money?

People saving money in banks or bonds know their money is safe. They know when and how much interest it will earn. When people **invest** their extra dollars, their money is not as safe. It might not earn as much. They could even lose money! People take this risk because investing may also bring much larger earnings.

Some people invest in costly things they collect. Some people invest in land or buildings. Many people invest their money by buying part of a company.

◄ *Some people invest in land or buildings.*

How Do People Invest in the Stock Market?

Small parts of a company are called shares of **stock.** Investors buy, sell, and trade shares in the stock market. This market can be a real place, like the New York Stock Exchange. It can also be business done just by computer.

Many people hire experts to help them invest. Some people invest their money themselves. Some traders, called stockbrokers, work full-time at a stock exchange. They usually do business for other people.

People may invest in a company because they know its **products.** Sometimes, people choose companies because they like the way they do business.

◀ *Stockbrokers work at the New York Stock Exchange.*

How Will People Save Money in the Future?

Some people already use computers to do their banking. Many stores and malls have automated teller machines (ATMs) for depositing and with-drawing money. In the future, even more saving will be done this way. Banks now offer accounts that people can use from home computers.

People are living longer. They will need to save more money for retirement. The Social Security Administration may run out of money. This could also change how people save for their retirement years. What do you think banking will be like when you retire?

◀ *An ATM is built into an elephant sculpture at the zoo in Bangkok, Thailand.*

Glossary

bonds—tools for long-term saving

credit union—a business that makes small loans to its members at low interest rates

deposit—an amount of money put into a bank account

expense—the cost of things used for living or doing business

insures—promises to pay an amount of money if something bad happens

interest—the extra money a bank adds to its depositors' accounts; also, the money a bank charges people for making loans to them

invest—using money in risky ways that may give greater earnings than just saving it

loans—money given to someone that must be paid back

products—things that are made or manufactured

reserve—to keep an amount of something separate and safe

savings and loan associations—businesses that hold the savings of their members and invest mainly in home mortgage loans

statements—reports of financial matters

stock—a way of dividing up ownership of a company; stock is owned and sold in shares

taxes—money collected and used by a government

wages—the money someone earns each week or month for the work done during that time

withdrawals—money that has been removed from a bank account

Did You Know?

- The word "bank" comes from *banca,* the Italian word for bench. Italian moneylenders would place coins on a bench when doing business.
- The first piggy banks were jars made from a kind of clay called "pygg."

- Before bank accounts were insured, people lost money when banks failed.
- About 55 million people own U.S. savings bonds.
- The first official bank in the United States opened in 1791.

Want to Know More?

In the Library

Godfrey, Neale S. *Ultimate Kids' Money Book.* New York: Simon & Schuster, 1998.

Otfinoski, Steve. *The Kid's Guide to Money: Earning It, Saving It, Spending It, Growing It, Sharing It.* New York: Scholastic, 1996.

Schwartz, David. M. *If You Made a Million.* New York: Lothrop, Lee, & Shepard, 1989.

On the Web

For more information about saving money, use FactHound to track down Web sites related to this book.
1. Go to *www.facthound.com*
2. Type in a search word related to this book or this book ID: 0756504848.
3. Click on the *Fetch It* button.
Your trusty FactHound will fetch the best Web sites for you!

Through the Mail

Young Americans Center
for Financial Education
3550 E. First Ave.
Denver, CO 80206
To find out how to start an account at its bank just for kids, Young Americans Bank

On the Road

Museum of American Financial History
28 Broadway
New York, NY 10004
Toll-free 877/98-FINANCE
To learn more about the New York Stock Exchange and the history of American finance; open 10:00 A.M. to 4 P.M., Tuesday through Saturday; closed holidays

Chicago Stock Exchange
1 Financial Place
440 S. La Salle St.
Chicago, IL 60605
312/663-2222
To see stockbrokers trade stocks in this busy marketplace and to watch a video explaining how the Stock Exchange works; open 8:30 A.M. to 3:30 P.M. weekdays; closed holidays

Index

About the Author

Natalie M. Rosinsky writes about economics, history, science, and other fun things. One of her two cats usually sits on her computer as she works in Mankato, Minnesota. Both cats enjoy pushing coins off tables and playing with dollar bills. Natalie earned graduate degrees from the University of Wisconsin and has been a high school and college teacher.